Model of Faith

LEONARD J. DELORENZO

MODEL

OF

FAITH

Reflecting on the
Litany of Saint Joseph

Our Sunday Visitor
Huntington, Indiana

Nihil Obstat
Msgr. Michael Heintz, Ph.D.
Censor Librorum

Imprimatur
✠ Kevin C. Rhoades
Bishop of Fort Wayne-South Bend
January 28, 2021

The *Nihil Obstat* and *Imprimatur* are official declarations that a book is free from doctrinal or moral error. It is not implied that those who have granted the *Nihil Obstat* and *Imprimatur* agree with the contents, opinions, or statements expressed.

Except where noted, the Scripture citations used in this work are taken from the *Revised Standard Version of the Bible — Second Catholic Edition* (Ignatius Edition), copyright © 1965, 1966, 2006 National Council of the Churches of Christ in the United States of America. Used by permission. All rights reserved.

Every reasonable effort has been made to determine copyright holders of excerpted materials and to secure permissions as needed. If any copyrighted materials have been inadvertently used in this work without proper credit being given in one form or another, please notify Our Sunday Visitor in writing so that future printings of this work may be corrected accordingly.

Our Sunday Visitor Publishing Division
Our Sunday Visitor, Inc., 200 Noll Plaza, Huntington, IN 46750, www.osv.com;
1-800-348-2440

ISBN: 978-1-68192-948-4 (Inventory No. T2683)
1. RELIGION—Christianity—Saints & Sainthood.
2. RELIGION—Christianity—Catholic.
3. RELIGION—Christian Theology—General.

eISBN: 978-1-68192-949-1
LCCN: 2021931664

Cover design: Lindsey Riesen
Cover art: *The Holy Family*, c.1660–70 (oil on panel); Murillo, Bartolome Esteban (1618-82) from Bridgeman Images
Interior design: Chelsea Alt

PRINTED IN THE UNITED STATES OF AMERICA

To John Cavadini,
whose devotion to Saint Joseph is displayed
in word and in action

Contents

■■■

Model of Faith

THE LITANY OF SAINT JOSEPH

Lord, have mercy.
Lord have mercy.
Christ, have mercy.
Christ, have mercy.
Lord, have mercy.
Lord have mercy.
God our Father in heaven, *have mercy on us.*
God the Son, Redeemer of the world, …
God the Holy Spirit, …
Holy Trinity, one God, …
Holy Mary, *pray for us.*
Saint Joseph, …
Noble son of the House of David, …
Light of patriarchs, …
Husband of the Mother of God, …
Guardian of the Virgin, …
Foster father of the Son of God, …
Foster father of the Son of God, …
Faithful guardian of Christ, …
Head of the Holy Family, …
Joseph, chaste and just, …
Joseph, prudent and brave, …
Joseph, obedient and loyal, …
Pattern of patience, …
Lover of poverty, …
Model of workers, …
Example to parents, …
Guardian of virgins, …

Pillar of family life, …
Comfort of the troubled, …
Hope of the sick, …
Patron of the dying, …
Terror of evil spirits, …
Protector of the Church, …

Lamb of God, you take away the sins of the world, *have mercy on us.*
Lamb of God, you take away the sins of the world, …
Lamb of God, you take away the sins of the world, …

God made him master of his household,
And put him in charge of all that he owned.

Let us pray.
O God, who in your inexpressible providence were pleased to choose Saint Joseph as spouse of the most holy Mother of your Son, grant, we pray, that we, who revere him as our protector on earth, may be worthy of his heavenly intercession.

Through Christ Our Lord.
Amen.

INTRODUCTION

BEHOLD

Behold, a faithful and prudent steward,
whom the Lord set over his household.
— Saint Paul Daily Missal

Jesus once asked, "Who is my mother, and who are my brethren?" and then he responded to his own question: "Whoever does the will of my Father in heaven is my brother, and sister, and mother" (Mt 12:48, 50).

Does Joseph do anything else? He is all hearing and all acting: he does the will of God. He is a brother of Jesus.

But that is not all Joseph is. He is also the only one among us who is also called father of Jesus. He does not call himself this; Mary does (see Lk 2:48). And God the Father entrusts Joseph with this very office: to be a father to Jesus.

In this devotional, I will at times call Jesus Joseph's "son." No saint aside from Mary has endured such an exalted honor. For a little while, the Lord of all was under the authority of this humble man. For a little while, the Son of the Most High took cover under the protection of Joseph. For a little while, Jesus was known as the son of Joseph.

The Litany of Saint Joseph takes us down a path of contemplation. We are led to contemplate the titles and honors of Joseph, husband of Mary and custodian of the Incarnate Word. To contemplate Joseph requires that we contemplate the mysteries of God, because Joseph, from whom Scripture records no words spoken, is directed by and responsive to the Word who speaks our salvation. To guide us in our contemplation, each of the following chapters focuses on one of the twenty-two names, titles, or honors of Saint Joseph, which we encounter in his litany.

What Scripture gives us explicitly about Saint Joseph is always in reference to the Word of God whom he heeded. He not only displays for us what obedience to God's Word looks like, but also reflects to us the wisdom of God's ways. The ways of the Lord are not our ways, but we must continually learn the ways of the Lord for our good and the good of all the Church. Joseph is both an example and an efficacious sign of the ways of the Lord. His life is his testimony, and his power is in his faith. To discern Joseph is to discern God's handiwork.

This is the man God chose to be as a father to his only-begotten Son. A sinner like us, Joseph was stretched in virtue and filled with the graces of God. God made him capable of this sacred duty — a duty entrusted to Joseph alone. Joseph is a singular figure in salvation history, and yet he shows each of us the way to respond to our vocations as disciples of Jesus and friends of God. He listened for God's voice and acted on what he heard, and he is thus a model of faith and obedience for all Christians. Listening for God's voice and acting on what he asks of us is the simple, demanding task of the Christian life. And as we see with Joseph, out of that simple obedience, God fashioned a great saint.

What do we gain by spending our days in the company of Saint

Joseph — praying with him, offering our petitions to his care, contemplating his life and his witness? What we gain is nothing short of being drawn closer to the mystery of God's dwelling with us.

Fostering a devotion to Joseph draws us into adoring Christ. Peter, James, and John once glimpsed the glory of Jesus upon the mountaintop, when their friend and teacher was transfigured before their eyes. Only later, upon the Resurrection, did they see this glory unveiled for all time. These three were great apostles, but apostles are still only servants of the Lord. Joseph and Mary were father and mother to the Lord. And rather than one day of transfiguration, they spent every day gazing upon the hidden glory of God's mercy drawn near to us. Indeed, in the beautiful words of Pere Binet:

> The entire life of St. Joseph was like a day of transfiguration, without any evening. Every day he contemplated the divine Face of the Infant Jesus; he beheld the white cloud — I mean his holy spouse, in which the Sun of Justice had concealed himself during nine months; he lived under the same roof with them. O how good it was for him to abide in that house more delightful than the terrestrial paradise, more holy than the Holy of Holies.

Jesus shares his life with us through his saints. From Joseph, Jesus received a father's love, and to Joseph, Jesus was an obedient son. For us, Joseph hastens to share the love he lavished on Jesus, and he yearns for nothing more than to draw us near to that blessed child, who is his and our salvation.

■ ■ ■

Saint Joseph, pray for us.

SAINT JOSEPH

... and Jacob the father of Joseph the husband of Mary,
of whom Jesus was born, who is called the Christ.
— Matthew 1:16

And Israel said to Joseph, "I had not thought to see your
face; and behold, God has let me see your children also."
— Genesis 48:11

Joseph was the son of Jacob. So it was in the time of the patriarchs, when Jacob loved Joseph best among all his sons. It was Joseph who received his father's special gift. It was Joseph who dreamed dreams, Joseph who labored and toiled to great success, and Joseph who fed and harbored the entire household of his father Jacob in the time of famine. Joseph brought all of Israel to Egypt to save them, and it was Joseph's bones that Moses carried out of Egypt when he led the people away from the Pharaoh who did not know Joseph (see Ex 13:19; 1:8).

Joseph was the son of Jacob. So it was again as the fullness of time approached, when Jacob's son Joseph would take Mary as his wife. It was Joseph who stood in the line of his father and his father's fathers, back to David and Abraham. It was Joseph who dreamed dreams, Joseph who labored and toiled in silent humility, and Joseph who fed and harbored the Savior of the world in days both of danger and of domestic tranquility. Joseph fled with Jesus and Mary to Egypt to save them, and it was Joseph who carried them home again when their exile came to an end.

Joseph, son of Jacob, husband of Mary and foster father of Jesus, fulfills the role of his namesake under whose custodianship all of Israel, and indeed the whole world, was saved from ruin.

Saint Joseph, the faithful custodian of the Word Incarnate and spouse of the ever-Virgin Mary, guards the treasury of the world's hope. Under his patronage, the blessings of God redound to a thousand generations. He watches Salvation grow.

Joseph of old brought the age of the patriarchs to a close. Saint Joseph held in his arms the One who makes all things new (see Rv 21:5). The old things did not pass away: the bones carried out of the past join together again, and flesh comes upon them, and a fresh spirit vivifies them, and all who have died are brought to new life through the child born unto Mary, wife of Joseph (Ez 37:1–14).

God does not forget his people (see Is 49:15), and his servant Saint Joseph is the witness to God's living memory. He is the first to behold the

> *Joseph, son of Jacob, husband of Mary and foster father of Jesus, fulfills the role of his namesake under whose custodianship all of Israel, and indeed the whole world, was saved from ruin.*

mystery of the Virgin who bears a child: God-with-us (Is 7:14). The patriarchs sought communion with God and the formation of a great people who would bear God's blessing. The child Saint Joseph cradled is the gift of that communion, from whom God's blessings pour forth for all who came before and all who are yet to come.

Joseph is the name of him to whom we can entrust our prayers. He is what he was called to be: husband, father. Tenderly, he stands by and comforts she who bore the world's salvation. Silently, he provides for the child who is Bread for the world. Simply, he directs us to Our Savior. Everlastingly, he offers our prayers to his son from his own fatherly heart.

■ ■ ■

Saint Joseph, you witnessed the dawn of our salvation. Pray that the love of Christ may dawn anew in our hearts and shine radiantly in our lives. Keep watch for us over the treasures that Jesus intends for us, and help us to become worthy of the promises of Christ.

NOBLE SON OF THE HOUSE OF DAVID

What has not been assumed has not been saved.

— Saint Gregory of Nazianzus

B y the testimony of Matthew the Evangelist, Jesus did not directly share in the bloodline of King David. Instead, the one who comes from David's line is "Joseph, the husband of Mary, of whom Jesus was born" (Mt 1:16). And the further testimony of Matthew, along with the testimony of Luke, confirms that Jesus was of Mary's blood but not Joseph's. Joseph gave his household but not his genes or his blood to this child born of the Virgin.

Rather than a point of regret, this is a point of glory. It is glorious that the Son of God, who is born of the Virgin, takes as his own what was not his by birth alone. Joseph gives to Jesus as his inheritance the nobility that Joseph possesses by his own birth. Because the Son of God accepts Joseph as his father on this earth, and because Joseph takes this child who was not his own as his own, Jesus comes to share in the royal line of David. As he is connected to David and, through David, all the way back to Abraham (see Mt 1:2, 6), Jesus takes his place in line of the history of Israel.

Joseph does not just give Jesus a place in the house of David; instead, he bequeaths to this child a place that exceeds his own and all others'. Jesus will be the head of this household, not merely a descendant. He raises up this household from history and unites it to the glorious household of his Father on high, from whose right hand he comes and to whose right hand he returns. This is what Jesus does with the inheritance Joseph gives him.

In this way, Jesus is grafted on to the royal lineage of the house of David. By his humility, he takes on what was not his own, as part of the flesh he took on when he descended from the Father. He received from Mary a place to dwell, flesh and blood, and a mother to call his own, both in spirit and in flesh. But from Joseph he also received the customs of his people, this particular place in the history of Israel, and a share in the kinghood of David, whose kinghood he himself would redeem.

> *Joseph gives to Jesus as his inheritance the nobility that Joseph possesses by his own birth.*

In the end, Jesus returns the gift he received from Joseph by sharing with all those whose lineage he inherits a share in the eternal lineage of his divine sonship. By this glorious exchange through the child he took into his own household, Joseph himself became a child in the household of God. So it was then, is now, and ever shall be, world without end. Amen.

■ ■ ■

Saint Joseph, you show us how to share all we have with this child, Jesus, and to trust that all he receives from us will be made new as he gives us a share in his divine kingship. You gave the name of your household to the Son of God, and in return he gave his own name to you, so that you yourself are raised up in him whose "name ... is above every name ... in heaven and on earth and under the earth ... to the glory of God the Father" (Phil 2:9–11).

LIGHT OF THE PATRIARCHS

Through the tender mercy of our God ...
the day shall dawn upon us from on high
to give light to those who sit in
darkness and in the shadow of death,
to guide our feet into the way of peace.
— Luke 1:78–79

Alongside his wife, Joseph presented the infant Jesus in the temple in Jerusalem, according to religious custom. He and Mary placed this child into the arms of the righteous and devout man Simeon, who had been waiting many long years for the coming of the Savior. Raising the babe heavenward, Simeon burst out in praise, declaring that hope had now dawned for all people:

Lord, now let your servant depart in peace,
according to your word;

for my eyes have seen your salvation
which you have prepared in the presence of all peoples,
a light for revelation to the Gentiles
and for glory to your people Israel. (Luke 2:29–32)

The child's father and mother marveled at what was said. Mary herself knew this child intimately from the first, holding him within her womb from the moment her *fiat* resounded throughout the heavens. She would ponder this child all her days, never ceasing to draw him deeper and deeper into her heart. But her husband, Joseph, came to marvel at this child from a distance. He did not share in the intimacy of Mary's unique maternal bond with the Son of God. And yet, he did not look away, as here, in the Temple, this unbearable light burst forth. This child — *his child* — was proclaimed as the light for the nations and the glory of Israel.

Joseph bore witness to what all the patriarchs from the beginning longed for. Here was God dwelling in the midst of his people. Here was God illuminating the darkness of sin and infidelity. Here was God sealing forever the covenant first initiated with Abraham, and before him with Noah, and before him even with Adam. Here was God blessing the whole world through the religious custom of his people Israel. Here was God: the very child he, Joseph, carried to the Temple several days after birth.

> *Joseph bore witness to what all the patriarchs from the beginning longed for. Here was God dwelling in the midst of his people.*

The wisdom of the wise ones of old is exceeded by the silent and chaste Joseph, who saw wisdom herself dawn that day. He beheld the wisdom of God; he basked in the light of God's coming. Joseph came as a poor man, offering the sacrifice of "a pair of turtledoves, or two young pigeons" (Lk 2:24) — the offering a faithful poor man would give. But the true sacrifice he carried that day was not these birds; it was this child.

Jesus was the sacrifice of God, given as light into the darkness of the world. Joseph, with his own eyes, beheld the light. He stood there as the last of the patriarchs, fulfilling what was begun long ago. The descendants the Lord had promised to Abram of Ur, who began from a distance to travel in obedience to the call of God, were completed and redeemed in the Son of God whom Joseph carried to the Temple that day. And like Abraham who would offer Isaac, Joseph handed over this blessed child in obedience to God and for the salvation of all.

■ ■ ■

Saint Joseph, pray that our eyes may behold the light you beheld. From however distant we may be, beckon us to draw near and marvel at this Good News. May we see the salvation of Jesus which Simeon proclaimed, which Mary pondered, and which you, most faithful servant and father, carried as a sacrifice of divine love in the presence of God.

HUSBAND OF THE
MOTHER OF GOD

*He was both the true and chaste spouse of the Blessed
Virgin Mary, and the foster-father of the Word
Incarnate. For these two reasons, Saint Joseph shines
among all mankind and approaches nearer than any
other saint to the holiness of the Mother of God.*
— *Pope Leo XIII*

How tender and strong she is, she who bore God. Tender, for she must receive with all sensitivity and delicacy the most precious gift, whom she allows to direct her thoughts and deeds, her words and dispositions. Strong, for she must carry a weight no other bears: the sweet and serious burden of bearing God in a world that loves him not. Tender and strong is the God-bearer, unique among all creatures as the one in whom the meaning of heaven and earth was hidden, through whom Salvation himself was born, and by whom the humanity that would be united to

God on high was given most generously.

To cherish the tender strength and the strong tenderness of her who bears the Son of God calls forth the most excellent fortitude, the most discerning sensitivity. How to honor and love her who bears such an awesome mystery, who gives all she has to receive this gift with unfailing generosity? This is the question that shapes Joseph's life.

To Joseph alone was the responsibility given to hold her who held God. From him alone was the utmost tenderness called forth to care for the tenderness that comforted "the Rock of my salvation" (Ps 89:26). For him alone was provided the strength necessary to withstand the trials and tribulations that accompanied Mary, whose mind and heart were conformed to the strong love of the divine Son. Joseph alone was betrothed to a virgin who became the Mother of God.

> *To wed himself to her who wed herself in faith and flesh to the Word of God, Joseph accepted a vocation that required nothing less than every bit of who he was.*

No doubt, he held her as she wept, and her tears fell for reasons surpassing his understanding. No doubt, he smiled when she laughed, even as her glee soared above his wildest imaginings. No doubt, he heeded the small tasks and large undertakings that are committed to any man who cares for his wife, and yet each of his deeds carried untold consequence for the life of the world.

To wed himself to her who wed herself in faith and flesh to the Word of God, Joseph accepted a vocation that required nothing less than every bit of who he was. But day by day, he stretched himself a little further from who he had been to become tenderer, stronger, bolder, and more sensitive through all those millions of ways that he was called to love this woman, and her alone. He was a husband like any other, married to a woman unlike any other. And by loving her for who she was and for who she became day by day, *he* became unlike any other. He became the husband of the Mother of God, by the faith pulsing through his flesh, coursing through his blood, dropping to the earth through his sweat and his tears.

■ ■ ■

Saint Joseph, you know the precariousness and the uncertainty of accepting a call you do not understand. Pray for us, that we, who often lack both knowledge of and confidence in God's call for us, may practice becoming tenderer and stronger, day by day. Help us to care for those entrusted to us as if they themselves were bearing God himself.

GUARDIAN OF THE VIRGIN

*God trusted Joseph, as did Mary, who found in
him someone who would not only save her life, but
would always provide for her and her child.*
                              — *Pope Francis*, Patris Corde, 5

B y the strength of his own virtue, Joseph guarded the virtue of
his wife. There are no shortcuts to integrity. Only the regular
and consistent exercise of both respect and reverence yields it.
Joseph not only respected and revered his wife's virginity; he also
respected and revered his own. And this because he was a man
who had given his whole heart to the Lord.

He is first among all to confess what the centurion later declared: "Lord, I am not worthy that you should enter under my
roof" (see Mt 8:8). Joseph's was the roof under which both the
Divine Child and the Blessed Virgin came to dwell. He knew best
of all that this was an honor and duty for which he was not worthy.

He required virtue exceeding what he possessed if he was to make a dwelling place befitting such precious company.

Joseph looked nowhere else to receive what he lacked than to the Lord, to whom he always responded quickly, ready to do his will. Joseph did not overestimate himself nor did he underestimate the Lord. In humility, he confessed what he lacked and received what he needed. Loving his servant's humility, the Lord provided him with what was required to respond to this sacred calling.

This is how the house of Joseph was built. It was built through humility and gracious acceptance. It was the house of virtue and of grace. He did not glance around to see what advantage he could gain from following the designs of others. He did not take his eyes off the family entrusted to him so as to flatter himself with other possibilities. He remained humble, confessing his limitations and his faults, ready to receive what the Lord gave and do what the Lord commanded.

Joseph did not seek kingdoms, but the Lord made his household into the dwelling place for the King. Joseph called his King "son," and the blessed reign of God was first expressed in the respect and reverence with which Joseph held the King's Blessed Mother. This respect — this reverence — was itself rooted in the respect and reverence with which Joseph held his own standing before the Lord, as both servant and protector. Joseph was meek enough to serve and yet bold enough to command the first earthly kingdom of the everlasting King.

The household of Joseph created the conditions in which

> *The blessed reign of God was first expressed in the respect and reverence with which Joseph held the King's Blessed Mother.*

a singular devotion to God was fostered. These conditions surrounded and guarded the Virgin. These conditions pleased the blessed and most royal Fruit of her womb. These conditions redound to the magnificence of Joseph, whose humility the Lord exalts, whose simplicity the Lord regales, and whose stability the Lord cherishes as a reflection of his own divine manner.

■ ■ ■

Saint Joseph, you show us that the good life is a life lived for the Lord, accepting of the responsibilities entrusted to us and caring for those entrusted to our protection. May we marvel at the beauty of the Virgin with eyes of love — with your eyes — so that we receive her anew each day as the precious gift who gives to us a Savior who reigns for ever and ever.

FOSTER FATHER OF
THE SON OF GOD

Behold, your father and I have been
looking for you anxiously.

— *Luke 2:48*

Before her son Jesus, Mary names Joseph "father." She knows quite well that this son of hers is not of natural human generation but was conceived in her by "the power of the Most High" (Lk 1:35). She knows that Joseph did not play a part in the conception of her son, and yet *she* names *him* "father." Ever obedient to the Word of God, Mary follows what the Lord ordains, and by the reckoning of divine rather than merely human wisdom, Joseph is appointed father to the Son of God.

With what graces must the Lord have endowed his servant Joseph to be as a father to the Savior born unto us? Indeed, the Father in heaven conformed Joseph to his own image, so that here below Jesus would see in the husband of Mary a reflection of his heavenly Father.

When Jesus posed a question to his disciples, it was Joseph who reigned in his memory as the example of fatherly care: "What father among you, if his son asks for a fish, will instead of a fish give him a serpent; or if he asks for an egg, will give him a scorpion?" (Lk 11:11–12). Joseph gave Jesus fish, and Joseph gave Jesus an egg. Joseph provided to Jesus what Jesus needed from an earthly father. And God the Father provided Joseph with the wisdom and generosity to care for his only-begotten Son.

Mary knew the secret of her husband. She knew that he was a man like any other man, and yet the one whom the Lord had appointed as father of this Blessed Child. In faith and through her own daily observations, she saw in her sweet Joseph the tenderness of God; she saw in her strong Joseph the power of the Almighty. And so she said unto her son: "Your father and I."

Still, all the while, Joseph never failed to marvel at the mystery of his own paternity. His paternity always was and always would be a pure gift, modeled upon and fully dependent on the fatherhood of God. The child whom he loved as his own son would, in response to his mother's words, say in response: "Did you not know that I must be in my Father's house?" (Lk 2:49). Jesus heard Mary call Joseph "your father," and in response he claimed God in heaven as his Father. Joseph heard both Mary and Jesus. He was indeed appointed father to Mary's son, but her son was in truth the Son of God. Joseph stood outside that mystery, yet was drawn into that mystery through Mary because God deigned it to be so. To Joseph alone, Jesus would always be "my son," and at the same

> *His paternity always was and always would be a pure gift, modeled upon and fully dependent on the fatherhood of God.*

time not his own. To the Father in heaven, Jesus was "my beloved Son" (Lk 3:22).

This is the marvelous mystery of Joseph's fatherhood: He claims this office with all the confidence and courage befitting one entrusted with this unique responsibility, and yet he yields to God the Father the right to claim this child as his own Son. Mary knows the link between Jesus' earthly father and his heavenly Father, and she confirms before Joseph and Jesus and the whole world the dignity and the beauty of Joseph's sacred office. And in turn, Jesus refers himself to his heavenly Father, which rather than detracting from Joseph's prominence redounds unto Joseph's favor. He whom Jesus called "father" is the faithful image of the Father whom we cannot see. To contemplate Joseph is to move toward the mystery of God.

■ ■ ■

Saint Joseph, you are father to the Son of God. Be a father to us. By your son, we are made children of God. Love us and care for us as if we were one with the child you received as your own. Offer us to the heavenly Father in the company of Jesus and with your beloved spouse, Mary.

FAITHFUL GUARDIAN
OF CHRIST

One trembling flame has endured the weight of worlds.
One vacillating flame has endured the weight of time.
One anxious flame has endured the weight of night.
— *Charles Péguy,* The Portal of the Mystery of Hope

God so loved the world that he gave his only-begotten Son. But the world does not love God. Christ is the light, yet "men loved darkness rather than light, because their deeds were evil" (Jn 3:19). Jesus was vulnerable from the start.

In a nighttime church, the small and quiet flame of a sanctuary lamp illumines the darkness. That flame, though powerful, must also be guarded lest the wind extinguish it and the darkness spread unchecked. So it was with the Son of God, who though possessing the power over heaven and earth submitted himself to infancy and childhood and poverty and the fickle winds of men's hearts. His saving mission was not to overwhelm power with

41

power; it was to suffer the consequences of the misuse of power by those who do not love God. In the fullness of time, Christ would allow himself to be extinguished so as to enter into the final darkness of the grave, where he would rekindle his light for all time.

> *While he was in the world and in his most vulnerable state — as an infant, as a child — Jesus Christ required the custodianship of one who would not hate God but would rather serve God in faith.*

While he was in the world and in his most vulnerable state — as an infant, as a child — Jesus Christ required the custodianship of one who would not hate God, but would rather serve God in faith. Joseph was that guardian who tended the sanctuary lamp of the babe born to Mary.

Joseph shielded the child Jesus from the winds of malice with his own body and protected the sacred flame that would set the world ablaze. The winds of malice came swiftly for Jesus. No sooner did Herod hear of his birth than the tempest of jealousy roared within. Humble though he tried to make his words sound to the magi searching for the newborn king, Herod could not quiet the fury beneath his words. The magi knew not to return to Herod, and no sooner did they leave Joseph and Mary than Joseph determined to take flight with his young family to Egypt. Must not the malice of Herod have reached Joseph through the visit of the magi? From them, he must have learned the sacred flame was in danger. And so when the angel whispered in his ear while he slept, Joseph was ready to listen and to act.

The trepidation of the magi was a sign of the times; the clarion command of the angel was the appeal to faith. Joseph did not dither and did not dally. He arose immediately and, with singular devotion, began to shelter the Light of the World from the encroaching darkness. With haste he fled, and the malice of Herod could not keep pace with Joseph's fidelity.

This faithful guardian of Christ was a buffer against the darkness. Under his protection, God's gift to the world grew. Night in and night out, Joseph kept watch, so that, when this little flame was fully grown, he would burst through the doors of the sanctuary and become the everlasting dawn.

■ ■ ■

Saint Joseph, did fear arise in your heart as you guarded our Savior? May the faith that preserved you be given to us so that we may, like you, withstand the trials of our days and protect what is most precious in a world that is still so full of malice.

HEAD OF THE HOLY FAMILY

*He employed his legal authority over the Holy Family
to devote himself completely to them in his life and
work. He turned his human vocation to domestic
love into a superhuman oblation of himself, his heart
and all his abilities, a love placed at the service of the
Messiah who was growing to maturity in his home.*
— *Pope Francis*, Patris Corde, 1

God qualifies those whom he calls, and so it was with Joseph. No patriarch or prophet, no king or apostle, was given the sacred office which Joseph alone assumed. He alone among men was chosen to be father to the Son of God and husband to the Mother of God. He was given paternal authority over him who rules over all; he alone could command him who commands the wind and sea (see Mk 4:35–41; Jb 38:1–18). He was made "one flesh" with her who was ever virgin and with whom he constructed a fitting dwelling place for the Lord.

Joseph's name is the roof over Jesus and Mary. When Caesar Augustus ordered the whole world to be enrolled, it was under Joseph's name that both were registered in the census. Under Joseph's name Jesus received a share in the most basic form of human communion: the communion of family life. Whatever the Son of God assumed was saved, and so under the name of Joseph family life becomes not just a site but indeed a source of salvation. The Son of the Most High humbled himself to take cover under the name of Joseph, while the mystery of Mary's motherhood was protected under the spousal care of her most chaste spouse.

> *Whatever the Son of God assumed was saved, and so under the name of Joseph family life becomes not just a site but indeed a source of salvation.*

Is any man large enough to give cover to the Son of God and his Blessed Mother? No, on his own and in his own name, no man could fit such great mysteries under his roof. But the prayer of the psalmist was directed toward Joseph, who was made fit to his calling by the Lord's own blessing:

> Lift up your heads, O gates!
> and be lifted up, O ancient doors!
> that the King of glory may come in. (Psalm 24:7)

God the Father blessed his servant Joseph, making him capable of his role as head of the Holy Family. In his cooperation with grace, Joseph became the husband fit to the Virgin Mary and the father fit to the Christ Child. He became what they needed him to be through an unending prayer of humility and trust: "The house of my soul is too small for you to enter [O Lord]: make it more spacious by your coming."

Joseph's soul was expanded and his humble name was enlarged so as to cover over the world's Salvation. His arms held the Son of God and his Blessed Mother, and his household was a dwelling place for heaven on earth. He built and ruled over the household of the Holy Family because he allowed himself to be continually built and ruled by the power and wisdom of God (see 1 Cor 1:24).

Joseph was transformed by those whom he loved, by those whom he protected, by those whom he cared for, and by those who took his name as their own. Jesus and Mary were imprinted on him so that he has became a living icon of God-with-us. "Open the heart of Joseph, and you will find therein the fruitful copies, the perfect imitations of the sublime virtues of his adopted son Jesus, and of his blessed spouse Mary."

■ ■ ■

Saint Joseph, your name became great because you gave everything to the Lord. Hasten by your prayers to our aid, that we may relinquish our desires for worldly greatness and give ourselves generously to the Lord, who builds up the humble and exalts the lowly.

JOSEPH, CHASTE
AND JUST

When his mother Mary had been betrothed to Joseph,
before they came together she was found
to be with child of the Holy Spirit.
— Matthew 1:18

The use of the passive voice is curious in the above Scripture passage: "She was found to be with child." Surely, Mary told Joseph. If her pregnancy were widely known, the discretion of Joseph in planning to "send her away quietly" would be for naught. The passive voice leads us away from focusing on Mary, who actively disclosed the pregnancy, and leads toward the one who received this most unexpected and troubling news: Joseph. What occurred was not his action; instead, in his eyes, he beheld his betrothed who had changed and, from his perspective, "she was found to be with child." Joseph was the recipient of this mystery — he was not yet part of it.

Joseph was, as the evangelist Matthew attests, "a just man" (1:19). The evidence of his character was displayed in his desire to protect his betrothed from the shame that would fall upon her should her pregnancy become known. Mary would in fact be in grave danger for conceiving a child outside of marriage. It is not difficult to imagine the fury and humiliation that would flare up within any man in Joseph's situation, and yet this is the very first thing the evangelist says about Joseph after announcing Mary's mysterious pregnancy: he was a just man, and he wanted to protect her from shame.

Joseph's instinct, it seems, was not to act for himself but rather for Mary. In regard to her pregnancy, he had been passive, but in response to her situation, he immediately took action. The just man cares not for what is due to him first and foremost, but rather for the good of others. Joseph showed his quality from the start: his instinct was to protect, to guard, to aid and support. How did Joseph's transition from passive recipient to active agent look to God?

Though it takes us outside the boundaries of what we can know or even imagine, might we merely wonder if God had looked down upon this "just man" and was well pleased? Joseph received clarity for and confirmation of his call when the angel came to him in a dream, but that happened after Mary "was found to be with child" and Joseph "resolved to send her away quietly." Here was a man ready to work with God in the plan of salvation. Might we wonder if God sending his angel to Joseph was his way of saying, "Well done, good and faithful servant; you have been faithful over a lit-

> *Joseph was chaste as well as just, and his chastity inclined him to relinquish his own designs and heed God's designs.*

tle, I will set you over much" (Mt 25:21, 23; see Lk 16:10)?

The "much" over which God set Joseph was *very* much indeed. This is the man whom God chose to shelter his only-begotten Son and his Blessed Mother. He whose instinct was to lay aside his own claims in order to guard and protect was set over the dwelling place of God-with-us.

Joseph was directed to enter fully into marriage with Mary, with whom he would become "one flesh" and give life. The fecundity of their marriage would not be through conjugal procreation, but rather through the spousal love that nurtured a domestic life for the Author of Life himself. Indeed, Joseph was chaste as well as just, and his chastity inclined him to relinquish his own designs and heed God's designs. And yet, in Joseph God had found a man after his own heart (see 1 Sm 13:14). Like his Creator, Joseph would not seek to dominate and control, but to nurture and shelter and love.

Joseph showed his quality, and the Lord blessed him abundantly, entrusting this chaste and just man with what is most precious of all.

■ ■ ■

Saint Joseph, you were free of the lust for power and status — free to love generously. Pray that we may become trustworthy in the small things set before us so that, in the Lord's good time, we may become worthy of being set over the greater things that hasten the coming of God's kingdom on earth.

JOSEPH, PRUDENT
AND BRAVE

Who then is the faithful and wise servant,
whom his master has set over his household,
to give them their food at the proper time?
— *Matthew 24:45*

Joseph was not hasty, and he did not delay. He was, in a word, prudent.

Like his namesake in the Book of Genesis, Joseph is a dreamer. Three times and then continuing into a fourth, Joseph dreams during the infancy of Jesus. It is easy to focus so much on the content of those dreams and the supernatural spectacle we imagine each one to be that we miss what comes before and what comes after. It is in the before and after that we see the prudence and then the bravery of Joseph, which distinguish him from even the patriarch Joseph of Genesis.

In his first dream, an angel counsels Saint Joseph against fear and instructs him to take Mary as his wife (see Mt 1:20–21). In the second, an angel tells Joseph to flee with his family to Egypt to escape the wrath of Herod (2:13). In the third and continuing into the fourth dream, an angel directs him to return to his homeland upon Herod's death, and then redirects him from Judea to Nazareth in Galilee to avoid Herod's successor (2:20, 22). If only an angel would appear to me — we might each think — then I would know exactly what to do in uncertain situations. But it is not so simple. Joseph is not just passively moved around; instead, he prepares for and responds to the angelic counsels.

In each instance, Joseph is aware of and attentive to what is going on around him. First, he has learned of Mary's pregnancy, and "he considered this" (1:20). He is heeding the circumstance and deliberating on it. He had resolved to treat Mary kindly, but then, in his dream, further clarity comes to him as "he considered this," and so "when Joseph woke from sleep, he did as the angel of the Lord commanded him" (1:24). He did not act too hastily when confronted with this most unexpected pregnancy, but when clarity was given him, he acted immediately, without delay.

Second, after the visit of the wise men, who were themselves warned not to return to Herod in a dream, Joseph himself dreams and knows he, too, should flee from Herod. Though Scripture is silent on this point, is it not completely reasonable to assume that the wise men told Joseph of their suspicions about Herod before they set out for home by a different route? Certainly Joseph, who previously "considered" Mary's unexpected pregnancy, also considered this circumstance and mulled over in his mind what this meant for the child now entrusted to his care. When clarity came through the angelic counsel in his dream, Joseph "rose and took the child and his mother by night, and departed to Egypt" (2:14). Here again, Joseph deliberated in the face of this unanticipated situation and then, when clarity came, he acted immediately, without delay.

Third, Joseph remained patient in the foreign land of his exile, where he kept his wife and child in hiding until the danger passed. He refrained from acting prematurely according to his own whims or wishes, exercising instead the restraint necessary to wait upon the word of the Lord. Only once the angel came to him a third time did he rise and take "the child and his mother, and went to the land of Israel" (2:21). In this instance, and each of the previous two, Joseph acted immediately once clarity was given to him, but not before.

Is this not a most remarkable thing? Here is a man who looks squarely at his situation, refusing to shy away from what is going on, but who waits for clarity to dawn before making his move. And yet, the instant clarity is given, he does not delay but promptly acts without further questioning. Here is a glimpse of the bravery of Joseph, whose power over evil flows from his obedience to the Lord upon whom he waits. He is the image of prudence: that rare and precious virtue that demands forthrightness in reckoning with circumstances, patience in deliberating how to act, and promptness in acting once clarity dawns. One imprudent man is hasty in acting prematurely, while another is slow to act when the time comes. Only one who is patient then resolved is fully prudent, as was Saint Joseph to whom clarity was given while he slept.

> *The instant clarity is given, he does not delay but promptly acts without further questioning.*

The patriarch Joseph of ancient Israel did not begin with the prudence of the foster father of Jesus. He had to learn prudence through what he suffered. When Joseph in Genesis began to dream, he was overly hasty in interpreting his own dreams and foolish in telling what he had seen to his brothers. In time, Joseph would be the one who preserved the life of all his brothers and his father's household, but when he saw images of this mission in his dreams, he supposed that he would be exalted so they all would have to revere him — almost worship him. He was not patient in learning to see that he was to be lifted up so that he might serve and feed his brothers, who would come in need to Joseph (see Gn 37:5–11 and 50:18–21). While Joseph lacked prudence, he remained naive and pompous; only when the patriarch Joseph become prudent did he display true bravery.

It is not enough to marvel at the angelic counsels given to Saint Joseph, because then we would miss the discipline, virtue, and readiness that permitted him to receive and respond to the angelic counsels aright. A man of prudence is truly brave, and a brave man is truly prudent. Such is Saint Joseph, who cooperated with wisdom of God.

■ ■ ■

Saint Joseph, you did not hide from the circumstances surrounding you, and yet you did not act too quickly on your impulses. You, who wait for the Lord and follow him when he calls, pray that we may develop the discipline and the willingness of one who is a friend of God, trusting in his ways. Pray, we beg you, that we fill ourselves with the prudence and bravery that you exercised to the full.

Joseph, Obedient
and Loyal

In every situation, Joseph declared his own
"fiat," like those of Mary at the Annunciation
and Jesus in the Garden of Gethsemane.
— *Pope Francis,* Patris Corde, 3

For human beings like us, there is no question as to whether or not we will be influenced. We are shaped and formed, guided and directed by what surrounds us and what we heed, whether consciously or subconsciously. What we constantly look at and listen to influences us. Joseph was no different from anyone else in this regard. He was shaped and formed, guided and directed. What sets Joseph apart is that he was in command of his influences.

Commanding his influences means that Joseph exercised the discipline and the wisdom to decide what would influence him and what would not. Cultivating this discipline is a matter of determining what you regularly heed, pay attention to, and surround yourself with. Joseph was, first and foremost, a man whose ear was always open to the voice of God and whose eyes were trained to seeing the Lord's signs. Then, he acted on what the Lord commanded.

"Listen carefully, my son, to the master's instructions, and attend to them with the ear of your heart." So begins the Rule of Saint Benedict, written to guide and shepherd those who seek the Lord to grow toward union with him. Joseph is a model of what Benedict imagines: He displays the magnificent beauty of attending to the Lord with the ear of his heart. This listening is no shallow hearing; rather, it is deep and rich — a listening that takes root in the heart and directs his actions, and indeed, his entire life. As Saint Benedict continues, "The Lord waits for us daily to translate into action, as we should, his holy teachings." From the open and attentive heart, the task of the Lord's servant is to then translate what he hears into action. Joseph is all action: He acts on the Word of the Lord.

Few are the actions attributed to Saint Joseph in Scripture, but each one is a bold declaration of trust and fidelity. In Matthew's Gospel, he hears the counsels of the angelic messenger, and each time he acts immediately upon the instructions. In Luke's Gospel, he travels with his betrothed and abides with her as she gives birth; he listens as the shepherds proclaim the angelic announcement they themselves received; he submits his son for religious customs; and he seeks and then listens to his son in the Temple when he proclaims that he must be in his Father's house. Everything about Joseph revolves around Mary and the child born unto her. Everything about Joseph is a testament to heeding the Word of God.

> *Everything about Joseph is a testament to heeding the Word of God.*

Joseph is loyal to one voice above all. There are other influences — within him and outside him — that would plead for his attention and seek to shape his desires and deeds. But Joseph is in command of his influences. He puts the Lord first. He gives the ear of his heart to his God. And out of that loyalty, by which he treats God as God, all his other loyalties fall into place. His loyalty to his wife is an expression of his loyalty to God. Even his loyalty to the child entrusted to him emerges from his heart which is fixed in his love of the Lord. In loving his child, his love for the Lord becomes complete: love made flesh.

A god is what you place your ultimate trust in, what you give priority to in your life, and what you treat as first and most important. Many profess belief in one god with their lips but worship another god in their heart. Joseph, whose words are recorded nowhere in Scripture, proves whom he worships through his actions. He listens to and follows the God of Abraham, Isaac, and Jacob — the God of Jesus Christ.

The obedience of Joseph is in his consistency to listen and his promptness to act, while his loyalty is in remaining obedient to the same voice at all times. Joseph's house is in order: It is a house that serves the Lord (see Jos 24:15).

■ ▪ ■

Saint Joseph, pray that we may be put in order so as to love God with all our heart, all our soul, all our strength, and all our mind, and then show that love by loving our neighbors as ourselves.

PATTERN OF PATIENCE

Love is patient.
— 1 Corinthians 13:4

The first thing that Saint Paul says about love in his unforgettable reflection in the first letter to the Corinthians is that "love is patient." Patience is the first thing, as if to say that without patience, there can be no love. Paul is not making his own claim here; rather, he is following the pattern that God himself establishes. God establishes the pattern of patience, Paul sings of this pattern, and Saint Joseph is completely conformed to this pattern.

The Greek term that Saint Paul employs in 1 Corinthians 13:4, translated into English as "patience," is *makrothyméi*. This Greek term is itself a translation of a Hebrew term found in Exodus 34:6, and that Hebrew term is *'erek 'appayim*. The context of this term in Exodus is the Lord's own speech, where God gives an account of himself — of who he is — to Moses:

The LORD passed before [Moses] and proclaimed, "The

61

Lord, the Lord, a God merciful and gracious, slow to anger [*'erek 'appayim*] and abounding in mercy and faithfulness." (Exodus 34:6)[1]

When Paul opens his great hymn by stating that "love is patient," he is not simply translating a term from Hebrew to Greek (which for us is then further translated into English). Paul is also translating a divine attribute into human life. In the one who practices love as being "slow to anger," divine love is taking flesh. This is a form of participation in God's own way of being — participation in divine life.

In Exodus 34, God reveals himself as the one who is "slow to anger" in being patient with sinners. The sinners here are actually a sinful nation — the nation of Israel — who have turned their backs on the Lord and worshiped an idol of their own making. God does not wipe them out, as is their due. Instead, God opens up the possibility of repentance. God waits, giving these sinners the gift of time.

In waiting, God does two things at once. On the one hand, God withholds the just power to strike at sinners so that they immediately feel the full effect of their sin. On the other hand, God reveals what true power is, since in patience — "slow to anger" — God is not consumed by compulsion or passion, but rather chooses to create the time and space for new possibilities to arise for his sinful creatures. Out of their sinful rejection of God, God creates anew. God's patience is the source of hope.

Patience is the power to restrain yourself, even setting aside your just due, in order to grant unto others the possibility to change and to grow. Patience is discipline and creativity: the discipline to refrain from acting too quickly and the creativity to create the time and space for something new. Only the one who is patient can truly love, because patience is necessary for willing the

---

1. Cf. Nm 14:8; Wis 11:23; 12:2; 15:1; Ps 86:15; 103:8; 145:8.

good of the other.

Saint Joseph created a home for the Immaculate Virgin and the Son of God. Those with whom he lived were without sin: his son because of his eternal union with his Father and the Spirit, and his wife in her unceasing communion with her son. How can any man love well enough a wife like this and this son who is an inexhaustible mystery? How could any man be worthy? "With men this is impossible, but with God all things are possible" (Mt 19:26).

God, who refrains from justly wiping out the impious and who creates the time and space for repentance, forms his chosen servant according to his own divine pattern. To make Saint Joseph fit for the call he alone receives to be spouse of the Immaculate Virgin and father to the Son of God, the Lord conforms Joseph to the pattern of patience that the Lord himself designs. As God deals lovingly with sinners, so Joseph will overcome sin through God's help to deal lovingly with him who takes away the sins of the world and her who is the first redeemed among men and women. Only he who is patient is capable of love, just as love proves itself in patience. The Lord makes Joseph capable of love and proved his own divine handiwork in this man who became a model of patience in God's own fashion.

> *The Lord made Joseph capable of love and proved his own divine handiwork in this man who became a model of patience in God's own fashion.*

The home Saint Joseph created is a home of discipline and creativity. He himself is reserved so as to wait upon the mystery unfolding with his wife and child. He himself is creative in continually opening up the space and time for his child to grow to his full stature and prepare for his great mission. In his patience,

Joseph creates the conditions for God's loving kindness toward a sinful world to slowly ripen, preparing the young Jesus to venture out into a world that loves him not. The patience of Joseph makes room in an impatient world for the Son of God to begin to make all things new.[2]

■ ■ ■

Saint Joseph, hold us back from our anger and impertinence, and spur us onward in our regard for the well-being of others. Pray that we, too, may become enclaves of patience in an impatient world, as we allow God's love to come to full fruition in us.

---

2. This reflection relies, in part, on a section from Leonard J. DeLorenzo, *What Matters Most: Empowering Young Catholics for Life's Big Decisions* (Notre Dame, IN: Ave Maria Press, 2018), see 50–51.

LOVER OF POVERTY

And Jesus looking upon him loved him, and said to him,
"You lack one thing; go, sell what you have, and give
to the poor, and you will have treasure in heaven; and
come, follow me." At that saying his countenance fell, and
he went away sorrowful; for he had great possessions.
— Mark 10:21-22

The rich man was not free. He was a slave to his great possessions. He walked to Jesus looking for eternal life (see Mk
10:17), but he walked away from Jesus sorrowful. He could not
serve two masters (Mt 6:24), and the time had come to choose
between the two. One master sought to set him free, while the
other master wanted to keep him under control. The rich man
chose the latter: He became a slave to his possessions rather than
freely following Jesus from his heart.

Saint Joseph is all heart. He gave his heart to Jesus. Freed from
possessions, titles, status, and the esteem of others, he chose the
lot of the humble. He grasped after nothing, and so nothing had

a grasp on him. He did not love many things; he loved one thing. He loved the Lord. And that singular love made him a lover of poverty, for he loved *nothing* before the Lord.

To love poverty means relying on the beneficence of another. This is Saint Joseph. He does not store away resources to ensure his own security; instead, he entrusts himself wholeheartedly to the Lord. He treasures the Lord's protection and "happy are those who take refuge in him" (Ps 34:9, NRSV). Joseph loves lacking all he might claim as his own because "those who seek the LORD lack no good thing" (Ps 34:11, NAB). His hands are empty: He is ready to receive.

With what do you weigh yourself down, rich man? To what do you enslave yourself? Is it to a certain level of comfort that you have become accustomed and cannot do without? Is it from the opinion of others that you cannot break away? Is it the ability to rescue yourself from unforeseen hardship that you cannot let go of? Is it the delight in finer things that draws you back again and again, seeking more and more? These are weights that Saint Joseph threw off, accepting instead the yoke that is easy and the burden that is light (see Mt 11:30). Rather than the enchantments of all these illusory pleasures that would enslave him, he embraced from the start the one who sets captives free (Is 61:1; Lk 4:18).

> *Freed from possessions, titles, status, and the esteem of others, he chose the lot of the humble. He grasped after nothing, and so nothing had a grasp on him.*

The actions and office of Saint Joseph are together a mirror in which the whole Christian life is reflected. By what he does, Joseph shows that nothing is to be preferred to the Lord. By what the Lord entrusts to him, Joseph testifies to the daily duty of offering his heart to serve the Lord. He does so as father; he does so as husband. He does so from his particular station, which is the station of a humble servant whose treasure is stored up with the Lord in heaven.

The Lord has a claim on Joseph's heart — a heart which is set on the things above, not on the things below (see Col 3:2). And because his heart is kept safe above, he is free to move about and serve the Lord below. He is not burdened, and he is not a slave. He is a free man, who follows the Lord willingly, with all his heart, all his soul, all his mind, and all his strength (Lk 10:27). He is rich in this one thing and poor in all else. It is a matter of love.

■ ■ ■

Saint Joseph, pray that we may be wise and practical, for nothing is more practical than loving the Lord, who yearns to fill us with all good things.

MODEL OF WORKERS

At the workbench where he plied his trade
together with Jesus, Joseph brought human work
closer to the mystery of the Redemption.
— *Pope Saint John Paul II*, Redemptoris Custos, 22

Creation is the work of God. Nothing in the world — unto the entirety of the world — exists except as God's handiwork. God's work precedes our being, as humans. The dignity of God's work precedes and secures the dignity of our life as his creatures.

In all those years when Jesus lived outside the world's eye in Nazareth, he was obedient to Mary and to Joseph (see Lk 2:51). He learned from and followed them. This would be true of any loving and dutiful child, of course, but Jesus was not just any child. He is the Incarnate Word whose ways are as high above our ways as the heavens are above the earth (Is 55:8-9). Nonetheless, and by the inscrutable wisdom of God, Jesus submitted himself to the care and instruction of his parents.

So it was that the Word of God himself, through whom all

things were made and without whom not anything that was made was made (see Jn 1:3), learned how to make things in the ordinary human fashion in his father's workshop. "Is not this the carpenter's son?" (Mt 13:55), the perplexed crowds later asked. It was by Joseph's profile as a worker that the Word of God himself was first recognized among the men and women of his time.

What dignity redounds to Joseph in having as his own apprentice the one through whom all things were made? How marvelous that in his loving condescension, the Lord of all would bend down so low as to learn how to work from a human father, like so many other children before and after him. The fruit of Joseph's hands was not exhausted in the woodwork he produced; indeed, the formation of the Son of the Most High was the ultimate work of Joseph's life. By his own hands and with his own skill he helped to shape the customs, habits, and manner of work of Jesus, whose mission was the work of redemption.

> *It was by Joseph's profile as a worker that the Word of God himself was first recognized among the men and women of his time.*

Joseph's work happens in secret. We do not see his shop, or his tools, or his skill on display. We do not see his son growing up near his workbench. We do not see the lessons. We do not see the mistakes. We do not see the transferral of skill from the master carpenter to the young apprentice. We do not see how Joseph was, for a time, put over him who reigns over all. We do not see the work of Joseph the Worker. All we see is the fruit of his labor. And as that young boy who bustled about Joseph's shop would say unto others when he began his own work: "You will know them by their fruits" (Mt 7:20).

The dignity of Joseph, the Worker, is made known through the resplendence of the child he raised as his own son. All that happened in secret in that obscure town of Nazareth under the labor of this one carpenter was revealed as wonderful and dignified and of incomparable importance in the life, death, and resurrection of Jesus. In his work, Saint Joseph collaborated with God.

■ ■ ■

Saint Joseph, you who know what it means to work, pray that we may be strengthened for our work. You who know what it is to labor but not receive praise immediately for your labors, pray that we may persevere when recognition is delayed or withheld from us. You who know that the most important work happens in silence, out of view of the eye of the world, pray that we might be content with the portion the Lord grants to us. And you who never shied away from either the secular or the sacred work entrusted to you for the good of your family, your community, and even the salvation of the world, pray that we might be diligent and courageous in fulfilling the work we undertake for the good of others and for the greater glory of God.

EXAMPLE TO PARENTS

And when they say his name in town, when they
talk about him, when his name gets brought
up, at some chance remark, it will no longer
be him that they talk about but his [son].

All together, it will be him and it will not
be him, since it will be his [son].

It will be his name and it will no longer be
and it will not be his name, since it will be
(will have become) his [son's] name.

And he is proud of it in his heart and he
thinks about it with such tenderness.

That he will no longer be himself but his [son].

And that his name will no longer be
his name but his [son's] name.

73

> *That his name will no longer be at his*
> *service but at his [son's] service. Who will*
> *bear the name honestly before God.*
> — *Charles Péguy,* The Portal of the Mystery of Hope

"Is not this Jesus, the son of Joseph?" (Jn 6:42). Might this be the greatest honor Joseph ever received: to be remembered as the father of this man, Jesus? So great is the temptation for all parents to make a child an extension of themselves. The temptation to craft the child in their own image, to make them into accessories to adorn their own persona, to want to direct them in the ways they themselves see best. But Joseph was not there when these men remembered him through his son. Joseph himself had died.[3] Yet Jesus remains, and the great transition is about to take place. Jesus, who was once known as Joseph's son, is about to become the man through whom Joseph will always be remembered.

If not for Jesus, Joseph would not be remembered. For a lesser man, this would be an assault on his pride. Joseph built nothing that outlived him by which he would be remembered for a generation, let alone through the ages. His reputation was local and was buried with his kin. He was obscure, simple, and, for our purposes, silent. When Jesus appears in public, he is all by which Joseph is remembered. Jesus is his legacy. But a father — a true father — could hope for nothing else. All Joseph's hopes rest in Jesus. When these men ask this question of Jesus' identity in astonishment, it will be one of the last times — if not *the* last time — that Jesus will be known according to his father's name. Henceforth, his father will be known through his name. This father who was so strong, so wise, so towering as a figure in his young son's life all those hidden years in Nazareth, shall now become small. The transition is

_____

3. So far as we know.

taking place: His life's work is complete. He has given everything so that his son may live and give life.

Joseph is the example to parents, whose sacred call is not only to join God in bringing into existence the children that, without you, would not be. The sacred call is also to endow your children with what is most true and most beautiful. The call is to invest in your children without expectation of return — to give recklessly, with only the hope that your children will become who they are called to become. You will die and they will live. Joseph died and his son, Jesus, lived and gave life — he even called life out of death. Jesus eclipsed Joseph, and from his heart Joseph sang for joy.

> *This father who was so strong, so wise, so towering as a figure in his young son's life all those hidden years in Nazareth, shall now become small.*

■ ▪ ■

Saint Joseph, guide all parents into the way of love by which they can endow their children with what is best, most beautiful, and true. Pray that they may be freed from the temptation to expect a return on their investment, other than to see their children exceed us in grace.

GUARDIAN OF VIRGINS

*The total sacrifice, whereby Joseph surrendered his whole
existence to the demands of the Messiah's coming into his
home, becomes understandable only in the light of his
profound interior life. It was from this interior life that very
singular commands and consolations came, bringing him
also the logic and strength that belong to simple and clear
souls, and giving him the power of making great decisions
— such as the decision to put his liberty immediately
at the disposition of the divine designs, to make over
to them also his legitimate human calling, his conjugal
happiness, to accept the conditions, the responsibility and
the burden of a family, but, through an incomparable
virginal love, to renounce that natural conjugal love
that is the foundation and nourishment of the family.*

*This submission to God, this readiness of will to
dedicate oneself to all that serves him, is really
nothing less than that exercise of devotion which
constitutes one expression of the virtue of religion.*
— Pope Saint John Paul II, Redemptoris Custos, *26*

Virginity is simple; it is not easy. It is both a state and a calling to abide in perpetual devotion, offering body and soul as a single gift of spiritual worship. As Saint John Paul II discerns, the sacrifice of Saint Joseph arises from his "profound interior life," which grows to encompass all his external activities. By his discipline of virginity, his body is integrated with his soul. He is one whole man, offered in service and love to "the demands of the Messiah's coming." That offering is indeed demanding.

Not merely as model does Joseph guard all other virgins who make a special offering of themselves to the Lord. He is also the guarantee and the surety of the beauty and efficacy of such a life. As a father who shows his child what is possible whenever his child fears the unknown or the perilous, Joseph goes ahead not only to demonstrate, but also to instill courage in those called to virginity, whether for a time or for the span of a life.

> *By his discipline of virginity, his body is integrated with his soul. He is one whole man offered in service and love to "the demands of the Messiah's coming."*

Virginity is a perpetual rather than an occasional state. So long as that call persists, the need for perpetuity and constancy abounds. Doubts loom before this calling, as does hyperawareness of one's own weakness. But Joseph, the father to whom the Messiah was entrusted, goes ahead, always. As a father, he not only demonstrates what at first seems daunting and unlikely, but also to instill within children the confidence to do great things themselves. Fathers are never just models, because their influence is efficacious. Their confidence and tenderness become, in their children, courage. And so it is with Saint Joseph.

The holy desire that arose like incense from Joseph's interior life left a sacred scent on all his comings and goings. That same fragrant aroma comes to delight and inspire those who follow along his way of virginity out of loving service to the Lord. Virgins go forth knowing that they have a father who sees them, and loves them, and guards them in all their ways. He has gone ahead to clear a path, to set an example, to give them courage.

■ ■ ■

Saint Joseph, help us to make of ourselves a pleasing offering to the Lord, regardless of our call or station in life. But most of all, bless and guard those called to virginity, who follow in the special way of sacrifice that you yourself heeded.

PILLAR OF FAMILY LIFE

God alone could grant Joseph the strength to trust the
Angel. God alone will give you, dear married couples,
the strength to raise your family as he wants. Ask it
of him! God loves to be asked for what he wishes to
give. Ask him for the grace of a true and ever more
faithful love patterned after his own. As the Psalm
magnificently puts it: his "love is established for ever, /
his loyalty will stand as long as the heavens" (Ps 88:3).
— *Pope Benedict XVI*

It is so easy to get caught up in the uniqueness of the Holy Family that it is hard to see what this one family reveals about every family. In the hiddenness and mundanity of ordinary family life — with its scores of daily duties and its thousands upon thousands of humdrum interactions — Jesus, Mary, and Joseph practiced together patience and kindness, while routinely turning away from irritability, resentfulness, and jealousy (see 1 Cor 13:4–7). What they practiced together became, through Jesus, the source of life and the wellspring of renewal for the entire world. This is what every human family is called to be: a source of life for others and a wellspring of renewal for a world constantly in need. Life and renewal begin with what is practiced together in the family home.

As Pope Francis writes in his encyclical *Amoris Laetitia*, "The covenant of love and fidelity lived by the Holy Family of Nazareth illuminates the principle which gives shape to every family, and enables it better to face the vicissitudes of life and history. On this basis, every family, despite its weaknesses, can become a light in the darkness of the world."

The light who shines even in the world's deepest darkness is the Word who "became flesh and dwelt among us" (Jn 1:14). This light was enkindled in the quiet of Mary's womb. From that moment to his own dying day, Joseph guarded this light with his own life. The light of the world born unto Mary was sheltered in the home Joseph established until that light radiated outward from the Holy Family to all Israel and to the Gentiles, and indeed to "all nations" (Mt 28:19; cf. Lk 2:32; Jn 8:12). The light, life, and renewal that begins in the Holy Family does not stay hidden, but spreads outward for the good of the world.

> *From the moment of his conception to the moment of his death, Jesus shared in the life of a family whose joy and sorrow was shared in the midst of a wider community.*

The Holy Family was never closed in on itself. From his birth, Jesus lived from, toward, and with the wider family of Mary and Joseph. Upon learning of her pregnancy, Mary went "with haste" to visit her "kinswoman Elizabeth" who was also with child (see Lk 1:36, 39). Jesus' parents assumed he was with their "kinfolk and acquaintances" when they left him behind in the Jerusalem temple (Lk 2:41–44). When Jesus was teaching in the midst of a crowd, someone told him that "your mother and your brethren" were trying to find him, with "brethren" likely meaning his cousins (Lk 8:20). At the foot of the cross, Jesus looked down to see "his mother, and his mother's sister, Mary the wife of Clopas, and Mary Magdalene," alongside his beloved disciple, John, who witnessed all these things (Jn 19:25). From the moment of his conception to the moment of his death, Jesus shared in the life of a family whose joy and sorrow was shared in the midst of a wider community.

The gift and the task of family life is to share in the life of the Holy Family. Through the family of Jesus, Mary, and Joseph, God offered the source of life and wellspring of renewal to others. Because God has worked his redemptive will through this one family, family life itself becomes an instrument of God's saving grace. The Lord has blessed all families by joining himself to the family of Mary and Joseph. Through communion with the Holy Family, every family is called to share in this sacred mission of making all things new.

■ ■ ■

Jesus, Mary and Joseph,
in you we contemplate
the splendor of true love; to you we turn with trust.

Holy Family of Nazareth,
grant that our families too
may be places of communion and prayer,
authentic schools of the Gospel
and small domestic churches.

Holy Family of Nazareth,

may families never again experience
violence, rejection, and division;
may all who have been hurt or scandalized
find ready comfort and healing.

Holy Family of Nazareth,
make us once more mindful
of the sacredness and inviolability of the family,
and its beauty in God's plan.

Jesus, Mary and Joseph,
graciously hear our prayer.
Amen.

COMFORT OF THE
TROUBLED

*I took for my patron and lord the glorious St. Joseph,
and recommended myself earnestly to him. I saw
clearly that both out of this my present trouble, and
out of others of greater importance, relating to my
honor and the loss of my soul, this my father and lord
delivered me, and rendered me greater services than I
know how to ask for. I cannot call to mind that I have
ever asked him at any time for anything which he has
not granted; and I am filled with amazement when
I consider the great favors which God hath given me
through this blessed Saint; the danger from which he
hath delivered me, both of body and of soul. To other
Saints, our Lord seems to have given grace to succor
men in some special necessity; but to this glorious
Saint, I know by experience, to help us in all: and our
Lord would have us understand that as He was himself
subject to him upon earth — for St. Joseph having the*

85

> *title of father, and being His guardian, could command*
> *Him — so now in heaven He performs all his petitions.*
> *— Saint Teresa of Ávila*

Teresa of Ávila is a saint to whom many turn for guidance in times of trouble and to learn the ways of the Lord. But to whom did Teresa turn? Above all, she turned to Saint Joseph, devoting herself to him as her special patron and protector, supremely confident in the power and generosity of his intercession. Teresa knew that we can trust Joseph with our troubles precisely because God the Father entrusted Saint Joseph with everything. He even entrusted Joseph with the authority to command his only-begotten Son. Joseph endured hardships and danger on behalf of the Son of God, whom he called his own son.

Joseph was troubled over Mary's pregnancy, but he acted in faith. He was troubled when there was nowhere for his laboring wife to lay her head, but he acted in faith. He was troubled when Herod sought his son's life, but he acted in faith. In the face of every trouble, Joseph acted in faith and hastened to serve the child entrusted to his care. With care, he directed this blessed child and exercised authority over him.

The Son of God does not relinquish anything that he assumed, and this includes his relationship with Saint Joseph, who was on earth a father to him. Joseph, who responded to all troubles with faith, responds

> *Joseph, who responded to all troubles with faith, responds now to all those who share their troubles with him, exercising the same trust in God that he always exercised.*

now to all those who share their troubles with him, exercising the same trust in God that he always exercised. This trust in God was in truth a response to God's trust in him, allowing and empowering him to command even his only- begotten Son. Jesus hears and responds to the prayers his father on earth offers him, just as he heard and responded to the instruction and commands his father on earth gave him while they dwelt together in Nazareth.

Teresa of Ávila believes that the Lord honors those who honor him. Among men, no one honored the Son of God more than Joseph, who is the only one among us to ever love the Son of God with a father's love. Teresa entrusted her own troubles to Joseph, knowing that he would hear and respond to her with the same fatherly love, convinced that he would give her the very best by offering her own trouble to his beloved Jesus, who always heeds the voice of his earthly father.

■ ■ ■

Saint Joseph, may we have the confidence in you that filled holy Teresa with comfort in the midst of every trouble. When our troubles are so great that we do not even know what to pray for, let this be our first prayer: that we may have the confidence to entrust our troubles to you, who shares everything with Jesus, your son.

HOPE OF THE SICK

If I touch even his garments, I shall be made well.

— Mark 5:28

By night Jesus prayed, and by day he preached and healed. During one of those many days, a crowd gathered to follow Jesus. Somewhere lost in that crowd was a woman who had been suffering from blood hemorrhaging for twelve years. For those dozen years, she must have spent nearly every moment of every day praying for healing, and as the years dragged on hoping against hope that she would be made well. But on this day, she caught a glimpse of the man who had been healing others, and without any other hope she chased after him to seek the health she so desperately needed. Making her way through the ever-denser crowd, she barely caught up to this preacher and healer, just close enough to reach for the last fold of his flowing garment. Without permission and absent any concern for proper decorum, she stretched out to brush her fingers against this piece of clothing. She touched something that was touching him, and by that exchange of touch, she was immediately healed (see Mk 5:24–34).

If it sufficed for this woman to fleetingly touch his garment once to receive the healing she so desperately needed, then "my God, my Creator, with what innumerable graces must not Joseph have been enriched from the heart of the Divine Child, whom he carried so often in his arms, lavishing on him kisses and caresses! When he slept on the breast of the holy Patriarch, can you doubt that He communicated to him the sweetest and most ineffable graces?"

> *How much more, then, must Saint Joseph, who clung to the child Jesus day after day, be blessed as an instrument of healing for the sick who reach out to him.*

The fabric that mediated between the faith of the hemorrhaging woman and the source of our holy longing was blessed enough to effect healing that day in the crowd. How much more, then, must Saint Joseph, who clung to the child Jesus day after day, be blessed as an instrument of healing for the sick who reach out to him. Joseph clung to his child more tightly than any garment Jesus ever wore. By faith and with fatherly devotion, Joseph wrapped Jesus warmly against the cold, strengthened him against the dark, and cushioned him on the hardest days. By night, he held Jesus while he slept, and by day he carried him as he worked.

It was by faith that the woman reached out to touch Jesus' garment. When Jesus found her, he said, "Daughter, your faith has made you well; go in peace, and be healed of your disease" (Mk 5:34).

If by faith any who are sick reach out to Saint Joseph, then it will be through him that comfort will come from the Divine Healer. Jesus learned what it was like for a father to dote on his child from Saint Joseph, who absorbed pain and gave love. In gratitude to Joseph for all the days that he wrapped Jesus in his arms, the Lord himself says unto all those who ask for healing through the intercession of Saint Joseph: "Your faith has made you well; go in peace."

By night, the sick will rest in the peace of Christ, and by day walk in his glory.

■ ■ ■

Saint Joseph, when we do not have the words to ask for the healing we need, hear then our suffering as its own plea. Be attentive to what ails us and join it to the prayer with which you ceaselessly wrap the Divine Child whom you once held in your arms and now hold as your Savior, and ours.

PATRON OF THE DYING

I am the resurrection and the life.
— *John 11:25*

Joseph held in his arms Jesus, whom death could not hold. The same flesh, the same body that Joseph kept warm and held close to his heart, was revealed in glory on the morning of the third day. Only the Virgin Mary embraced the resurrection and the life as tenderly, intimately, and confidently as Saint Joseph, patron of the dying.

Joseph shared his home and his life with Mary, whom Christians have begged and begged to "pray for us sinners now and at the hour of our death." In an unceasing stream of petitions until the end of time, the Blessed Mother receives these prayers in the beatific company of her Blessed Child. And at her side, as she gazes in mercy at all of us sinners who beg her to unite us to her son, is her most chaste and holy spouse, Saint Joseph, patron of the dying.

Joseph died before his son had grown and set out on his great three-year mission. Joseph was there in the beginning, when Jesus was conceived in Mary through the Holy Spirit, and he was there throughout Jesus' childhood, at least until age twelve, but likely longer. He was there to form and to raise this child whom he loved as a son. Alongside his wife, he poured his life into this child. He must have glowed with that special pride that only a parent can know when he has sacrificed time and again for love of his child, and he would not hesitate to do it all again a thousand more times so as to give his child the very best. But Joseph was not there to see his beloved Jesus in full bloom, as Jesus, now his own man, went off to do his life's work: his Father's will. Never has a father given more, and then missed more, than did Saint Joseph, patron of the dying.

Joseph knows the sorrow of death. He knows what it is like to let go and lose out. He knows what it is like to gaze upon his wife and child as vital power leaves his body. He knows that last look of love from his loved ones, knows the anguish of that unsweet parting, knows the feeling of thinking ahead to the future his son will have, which he himself will not glimpse, but for which he himself gave so much. He knows the gratitude of a life well-lived in obedience to God, even if that gratitude is tinged with sorrow for that life's ending. He knows a holy death, this Saint Joseph, patron of the dying.

Joseph knows the hope and the joy that overcome death. He held that hope and that joy in his arms. He raised the young man who, when full grown, would not turn away from death but go right into it, so as to raise from death all who were lost, all who suffered the penalty of sin, all who tasted the bitter parting that comes at the moment of death. He shared a life with the woman who was preserved from sin and would not die, but would be assumed into full communion with her glorified Son upon her own dormition. He who experienced a death just like all the rest of us also lived a life in the company of the Savior who would undo death and of the Queen of Heaven and Earth who would be the first fruit of the resurrection and the life. No one knows the sorrow and joy of a Christian death like Saint Joseph, patron of the dying.

Joseph sympathizes with us at the hour of our death. He hears the petitions his beloved Mary receives for all those seeking mercy below, whether those pleas are spoken aloud or offered from silent hearts. He knows our sorrow and our hope, even better than we do. He who lifted the young Jesus upon his lap is ready and willing to lift up the whole Church, with its sinners and its saints, to join in the company of his precious Jesus. He beheld the resurrection and the life as a child and is now beheld by him in everlasting glory, where he desires for us to join him. When our prayers falter and come to an end, he keeps praying for us as our spiritual father: Saint Joseph, patron of the dying.

> *No one knows the sorrow and joy of a Christian death like Saint Joseph, patron of the dying.*

■ ■ ■

Saint Joseph, remember to pray for us with your blessed spouse at the hour of our death, and teach us how to die well in the love of your beautiful Jesus.

TERROR OF EVIL SPIRITS

Lord, even the demons are subject to us in your name!
— Luke 10:17

Evil is parasitic toward the good. Evil's final triumph is in making those who are created good and called to goodness believe that they do not have any power, that they are stuck and without hope. Evil wants those who are good to stare at evil, paralyzed by it, overwhelmed and overcome by darkness and gloom. Every evil spirit seeks to divide those who are good from one another and from their God — and while isolated, to suffocate them. Evil spirits desire your downfall, making you think you are alone with nothing to do and nowhere to turn.

But Joseph foils evil's plan, reflecting evil's failure back to itself. For he, who was a sinful man like all other sinful men, did not allow himself to become mired in his sin. He did not rely on his own strength or try to go it alone. He did not stop cold in the face of encircling gloom, whether from a bloodthirsty tyrant or from doubt in his own abilities.

Instead, when the evil spirits set their sights on him, desiring to isolate him and render him hopeless, Joseph the chaste held fast to God's word, listening for the Lord's voice and ready to heed his call, especially in uncertain times. Joseph the just acted righteously despite the sacrifices it would entail for himself. Joseph the bold moved immediately to do something when the powers of the world sought to eliminate his child and snuff out his family.

Joseph the faithful reveals that evil is not utterly disempowering. It is all an illusion. Because there is always something the good can do: you can pray and you can act. You can hope, because the Lord hears the cry of the poor.

Joseph shows what any sinner may become if he but clings to the Word of God and seeks to do God's will. In every dark place and every shadowy condition, the light of God burns for those who love him. Joseph's fidelity gives rise to his courage, and because evil feeds on despair, it cannot stand in the face of courage. And so, before Joseph, the evil spirits see their own reflection: they see that they have no power because God's power is the only power, and that holy power filled Joseph because he welcomed the Word of God.

> *Joseph is the terror of evil spirits because through him God shows them that they have no power of their own.*

Joseph is the terror of evil spirits because through him God shows them that they have no power of their own. Their victory will never be complete. God overcomes even Joseph's sin through his mercy, and by his obedience to God, Joseph is made surpassingly strong. He is so strong, in fact, that God entrusts his own Son to Joseph's protection. Evil cannot stand fidelity; every evil spirit vanishes before Joseph's faith. This man stands tall.

We sinners are never alone, even though we isolate ourselves in our sin. God's mercy has come for us. We need only to welcome him as Joseph did, heeding his voice and acting on his commands. Then we shall become surpassingly strong, because we will be pillars of faith, standing tall.

■ ■ ■

Saint Joseph, you are the perpetual sign of the redemption of sinners and the defeat of all evil spirits. Help us to see the Lord in our darkest hours. Help us to trust in him when we feel as if we are without hope, and help us to love him when love seems furthest from our hearts. Guard us from the evil spirits who seek to silence us, and lift us up to Jesus to whom you faithfully gave everything you had to give.

PROTECTOR OF
THE CHURCH

Blessed are those who dwell in your house,
ever singing your praise!
— *Psalm 84:4*

The Church seeks only to be at home in God, and God seeks to be at home in his Church. The Church is who she is when she waits with Christ, remembers Christ, and works for the reign of his Father, on earth as it is in heaven. God's reign is dwelling with his people, and all the faithful who live in the communion of the Church become themselves "like living stones" of a spiritual house in which God dwells (see 1 Pt 2:5).

Joseph put a roof over the head of God-with-us. He built a dwelling place more glorious than Solomon's temple. His home was a tabernacle for the living God. What the Church longs to do, Joseph himself did in Nazareth: He made a dwelling place for the Lord.

But Joseph could shelter the Lord only because he had first come to find shelter in the Lord. What the psalmist observed was realized in Joseph:

> He who dwells in the shelter of the Most High,
>   who abides in the shadow of the Almighty,
> will say to the Lord, "My refuge and my fortress;
>   my God, in whom I trust.
> Because you have made the Lord your refuge,
>   the Most High your habitation,
> no evil shall befall you,
>   no scourge come near your tent. (Psalm 91:1–2, 9–10)

Joseph took cover under the Word of the Lord, whom he obeyed unhesitatingly. Against the storms of confusion and the winds of malice, Joseph waited on the Lord, and when the Lord spoke, he found that his servant was listening (see 1 Sm 3:10). As Joseph dwelt in the shelter of the Lord, the Lord built up his servant to shelter his only-begotten Son.

Joseph, who loved Christ with all his mind, heart, soul, and strength, and who sheltered the divine Child by his own labors and paternal care, extends this love lavishly to all those whom Christ claims as his own. Joseph loves the whole Christ: head and members. And as he guarded and tended and nurtured Jesus from infancy through childhood and toward adulthood, so he seeks to guard and tend and nurture the Church whom Christ gathers to himself. With his

> *With his prayers and special devotion, Joseph protects the Church as he once protected Christ.*

prayers and special devotion, Joseph protects the Church as he once protected Christ. Joseph offers nothing of greater value to the Church than his own devotion to the Lord. He himself became a "living stone" in the Lord's spiritual house, and with his fidelity to God he seeks to help fashion and strengthen all those called to be built up into a dwelling place for God. There is no other way to become fit for the Lord's dwelling than to hasten to find shelter in the Lord. Joseph's strength in building and becoming a dwelling place for the Lord comes from his willingness to dwell under the Lord's own protection. As a father, as a master builder, and as a friend and patron, Joseph teaches this saving lesson to the Church he guards and tends, nurtures and loves.

Our Lord Jesus shares everything with us. He gives us his heavenly Father as our Father, and he gives us his earthly father as our special protector and patron.

■ ■ ■

Grant, we pray, almighty God,
that by Saint Joseph's intercession
your Church may constantly watch over
the unfolding of the mysteries of human salvation,
whose beginnings you entrusted to his faithful care.
Through Our Lord Jesus Christ, your Son,
Who lives and reigns with you
in the unity of the Holy Spirit,
One God, for ever and ever.
Amen.

Epilogue
Well Done

Well done, good and faithful servant; you have
been faithful over a little, I will set you over
much; enter into the joy of your master.
— *Matthew 25:21*

Joseph was not faithful over little; he was faithful over much. He was faithful as spouse of the Blessed Virgin, as father to the Son of God, and as head of the Holy Family. He was entrusted with much, and in the fullness of time, God rewarded his faithfulness by entrusting him with even more.

Joseph is to be for us Christians what he was to Mary: devoted companion and constant support. He is to be for us Christians what he was to Jesus: guardian and protector. And he is to be for us Christians what he was to the Holy Family: steward of the sacred mysteries and caretaker for all in need.

The Litany of Saint Joseph invites us to contemplate the honor and humility, the magnificence and meekness, the sacredness and solemnity of God's friend, Joseph. To give our attention and even a piece of our heart to contemplating this holy man is to offer ourselves, through him, to Jesus, whom Joseph both cared for and served. Everything about Joseph points to Jesus, including his love for his blessed spouse, Mary. To spend our time with Joseph is to grow in intimacy with Our Lord and Savior.

Let us not hesitate to entrust our cares and our needs to Saint Joseph. He has been faithful over much. He will be faithful in his love for us. This is the joy of God's saints: to love those whom the Lord himself loves. The master's joy is allowing his saints to love us as God himself loves us: They taste God's love in loving us. We increase Saint Joseph's joy when we turn to him; he rejoices over us in the love of God, and God delights in the delight of Joseph his servant — and with him, God delights in us.

■ ■ ■

Hear us, Saint Joseph.
Pray for us, Saint Joseph.
Guard us, Saint Joseph.
Strengthen us, Saint Joseph.
Bring us to Jesus, Saint Joseph.
Thank you, Saint Joseph.
Amen.

Notes

Page 13. ***The entire life of St. Joseph was like a day of transfiguration. ... more holy than the Holy of Holies.*** Pere Binet, *The Divine Favors Granted to St. Joseph*, trans. M. C. E. (Rockford, Illinois: TAN, 1983), 88–89.

Page 45. ***The house of my soul is too small for you to enter [O Lord]: make it more spacious by your coming.*** Augustine, *The Confessions*, trans. Maria Boulding (New York: Vintage Books, 1998), 6 [I.6].

Page 45. ***Open the heart of Joseph ... his blessed spouse Mary.*** Binet, *The Divine Favors Granted to St. Joseph*, 38.

Page 49. ***Joseph was directed to enter fully into marriage with Mary, with whom he would become 'one flesh' and give life.*** For further reflection on the marriage of Mary and Joseph, see John Cavadini, "The Sex Life of Joseph and Mary," *Church Life Journal*, December 18, 2017.

Page 56. ***Listen carefully, my son, to the master's instructions, and attend to them with the ear of your heart.*** Benedict of Nursia, *The Rule of St. Benedict*, ed. Timothy Fry (New York: Vintage, 1998), 3 [Prologue].

Page 56. ***The Lord waits for us daily to translate into action, as we should, his holy teachings.*** Benedict of Nursia, *The Rule of St. Benedict*, 5 [Prologue].

Page 80. ***The covenant of love and fidelity ... of the world.*** Pope Francis, *Amoris Laetitia: The Joy of Love*, 2016, no. 66, accessed January 20, 2021, Vatican.va. Cf., ibid., no. 119, where Francis adds that, "In family life, we need to cultivate that strength of love which can help us fight every evil threatening it. Love does not yield to resentment, scorn for others or the desire to hurt or to gain some advantage. The Christian ideal, especially in families, is a love that never gives up."

Page 81. *Jesus, Mary and Joseph ... graciously hear our prayer. Amen.* Pope Francis, *Amoris Laetitia*, no. 325.

Page 88. *My God, my Creator ... most ineffable graces?* Binet, *The Divine Favors Granted to St. Joseph*, 33–34.

Page 101. *Grant, we pray, almighty God ... One God, for ever and ever.* Daughters of Saint Paul, *Saint Paul Daily Missal*, 2114.

About the Author

Leonard J. DeLorenzo, Ph.D., directs strategic planning, undergraduate studies, and the Sullivan Family Saints Initiative in the McGrath Institute for Church Life at the University of Notre Dame, where he also teaches in the Department of Theology. The author of seven books including *A God Who Questions* (OSV, 2019) and the coeditor of a couple more, DeLorenzo writes and speaks regularly on the saints, Catholic education, the biblical imagination, and the development of character, among other topics. He and his wife, Lisa, and their six children live in South Bend, Indiana, where they are parishioners at St. Joseph Church. Find him on social media at @leodelo2 or visit his website at leonardjdelorenzo.com.

You might also like

A Man Named Joseph
Joe Heschmeyer

What is it that Saint Joseph has to offer the Church — and each one of us — today? That's the question that *A Man Named Joseph: Guardian for Our Times* seeks to answer. To get there, author, podcaster, and blogger Joe Heschmeyer cuts through a lot of our misconceptions to see what the Bible and the earliest Christians really say about Joseph as a model husband, father, and saint.

■ ■ ■

Patris Corde
Pope Francis

In his apostolic letter *Patris Corde* ("With a Father's Heart"), Pope Francis reflects on Saint Joseph and his multifaceted role as a father. The purpose of this letter, Pope Francis writes, "is to increase our love for this great saint, to encourage us to implore his intercession and to imitate his virtues and his zeal." The OSV version includes additional prayers and a litany to the beloved saint.

**OSVCatholicBookstore.com
or wherever books are sold**